FOR UNTO YOU

LIZ LEMON SWINDLE

AND IT CAME TO PASS IN THOSE DAYS, THAT THERE WENT OUT A DECREE FROM CÆSAR AUGUSTUS, THAT ALL THE WORLD SHOULD BE TAXED. AND ALL WENT TO BE TAXED, EVERY ONE INTO HIS OWN CITY.

ND JOSEPH ALSO WENT UP FROM GALILEE, OUT OF THE CITY OF NAZARETH, INTO JUDÆA, UNTO THE CITY OF DAVID, WHICH IS CALLED BETHLEHEM TO BE TAXED WITH MARY HIS ESPOUSED WIFE, BEING GREAT WITH CHILD.

AND SO IT WAS, THAT, WHILE THEY WERE THERE, THE DAYS WERE ACCOMPLISHED THAT SHE SHOULD BE DELIVERED.

AND SHE BROUGHT FORTH HER FIRSTBORN SON, AND WRAPPED HIM IN SWADDLING CLOTHES, AND LAID HIM IN A MANGER; BECAUSE THERE WAS NO ROOM FOR THEM IN THE INN.

ND THERE WERE IN THE SAME
COUNTRY SHEPHERDS ABIDING IN
THE FIELD, KEEPING WATCH OVER THEIR FLOCK
BY NIGHT.

AND, LO, THE ANGEL OF THE LORD CAME UPON
THEM... AND THE ANGEL SAID UNTO THEM,
FEAR NOT: FOR, BEHOLD, I BRING YOU GOOD
TIDINGS OF GREAT JOY, WHICH SHALL BE TO
ALL PEOPLE.

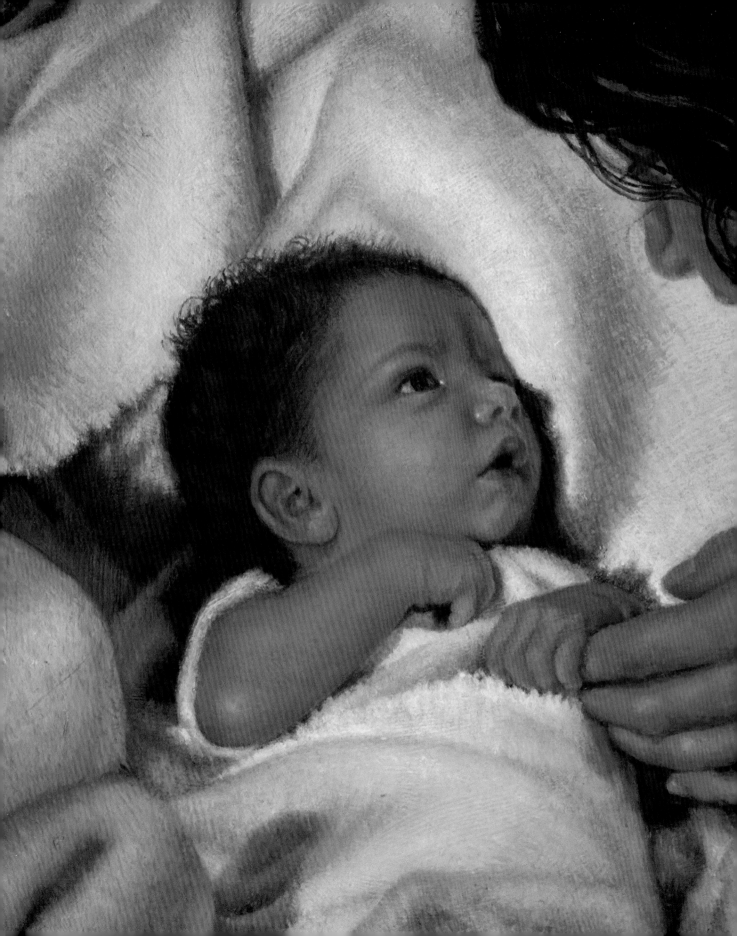

OR UNTO YOU IS BORN THIS DAY
IN THE CITY OF DAVID A SAVIOUR,
WHICH IS CHRIST THE LORD.

AND THIS SHALL BE A SIGN UNTO YOU; YE
SHALL FIND THE BABE WRAPPED IN SWADDLING
CLOTHES, LYING IN A MANGER.

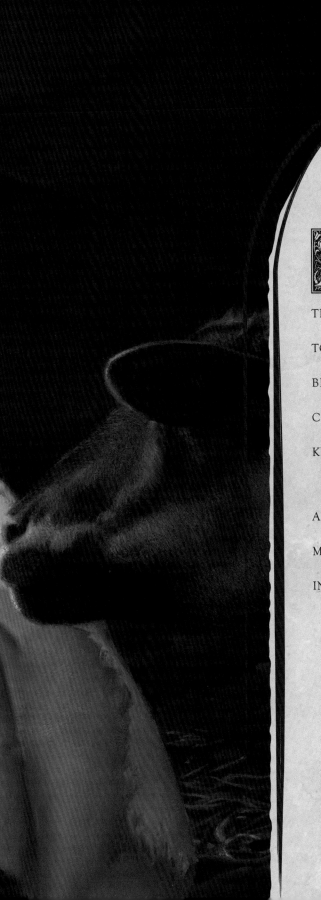

ND IT CAME TO PASS, AS THE

ANGELS WERE GONE AWAY FROM

THEM INTO HEAVEN, THE SHEPHERDS SAID ONE

TO ANOTHER, LET US NOW GO EVEN UNTO

BETHLEHEM, AND SEE THIS THING WHICH IS

COME TO PASS, WHICH THE LORD HATH MADE

KNOWN UNTO US.

AND THEY CAME WITH HASTE, AND FOUND

MARY, AND JOSEPH, AND THE BABE LYING

IN A MANGER.

UT MARY KEPT ALL THESE THINGS,

AND PONDERED THEM IN HER HEART.

LUKE 2: 1-19

OW WHEN JESUS WAS BORN IN BETHLEHEM... BEHOLD, THERE CAME WISE MEN FROM THE EAST...

AND WHEN THEY WERE COME INTO THE HOUSE, THEY SAW THE YOUNG CHILD WITH MARY HIS MOTHER, AND FELL DOWN, AND WORSHIPPED HIM: AND WHEN THEY HAD OPENED THEIR TREASURES, THEY PRESENTED UNTO HIM GIFTS; GOLD, AND FRANKINCENSE, AND MYRRH.

MATTHEW 2:1, 11

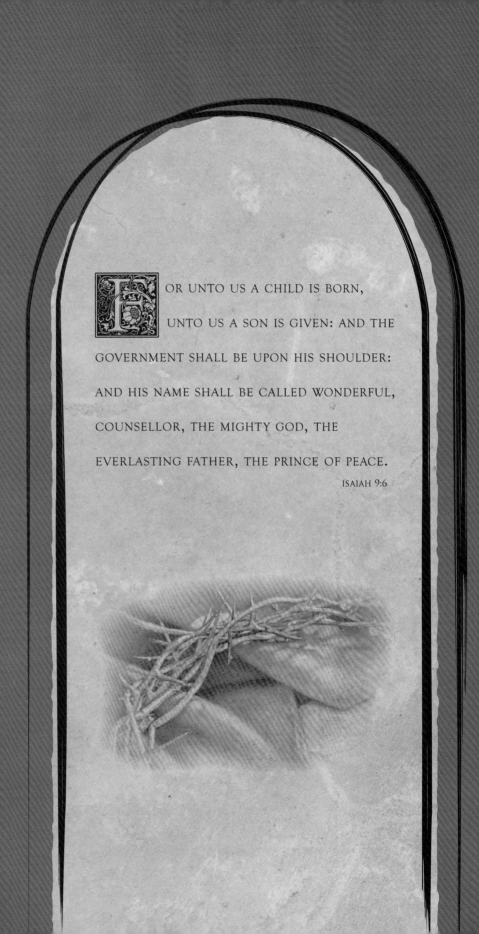

FOR UNTO US A CHILD IS BORN, UNTO US A SON IS GIVEN: AND THE GOVERNMENT SHALL BE UPON HIS SHOULDER: AND HIS NAME SHALL BE CALLED WONDERFUL, COUNSELLOR, THE MIGHTY GOD, THE EVERLASTING FATHER, THE PRINCE OF PEACE.

ISAIAH 9:6